The story of paper

MADE IN SOUTH AFRICA

Lynn Barnes

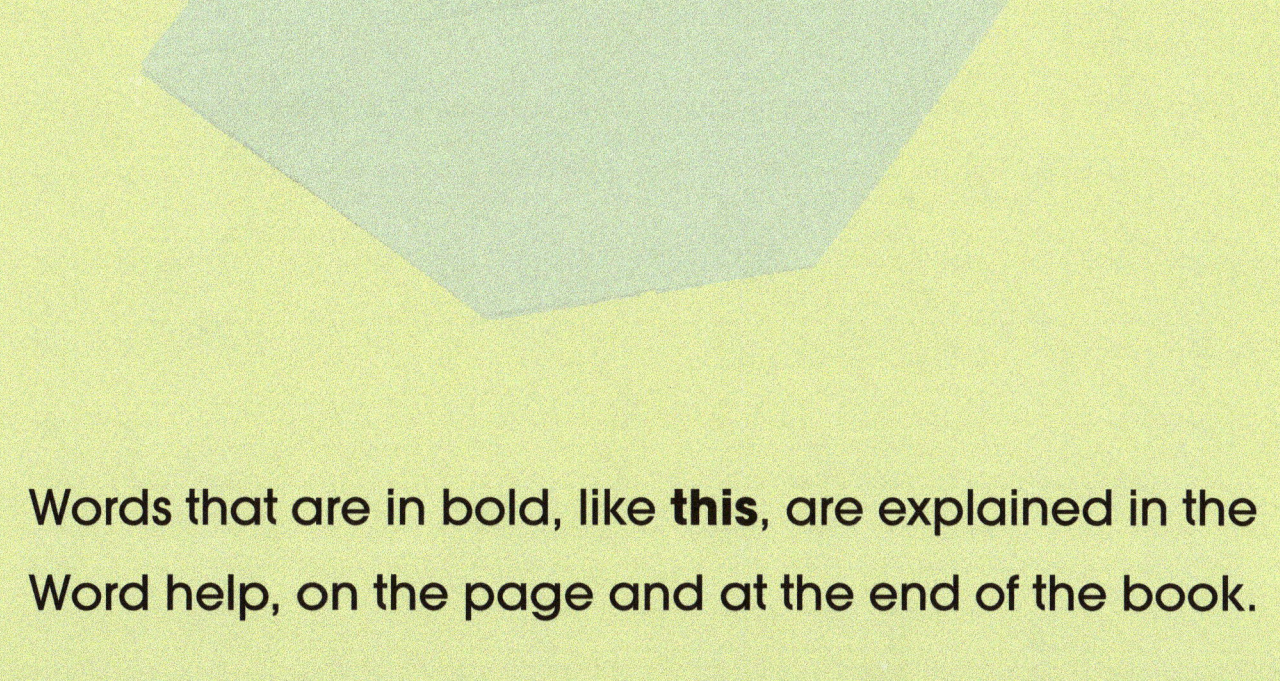

Words that are in bold, like **this**, are explained in the Word help, on the page and at the end of the book.

The *Made in South Africa* series is published by
Awareness Publishing Group (Pty) Ltd.
Copyright © 2019

Awareness Publishing (SA) (Pty) Ltd
www.awareness.co.za
info@awareness.co.za
+27 (0)86 110 1491
www.facebook.com/AwarenessPublishing

All rights reserved. No part of this publication may be reproduced in any form without written permission from the publisher, except by a reviewer.

First edition 2019

The story of paper by Lynn Barnes
ISBN 978-1-77008-992-1

Summary: A simple introduction to paper, explaining where it comes from and how it is made.

Book design: Richard Keenan-Smith and Elizabeth Barnard

Editorial credits: Managing editor: Monique le Riché; Copy editor: Danya Ristić-Schacherl; Picture editors: Anne Laing and Lawrence Frank

Picture credits: Cover © subman / iStock; cover (background) © Sappi; cover (flag) © Kurt / Dreamstime; endpapers © subman / iStock; p4 © Anne Laing; p6 © Delpixart / iStock; p8 © Roger de la Harpe / Africa Media Online; p9 © AAI FotoStock SA / Alamy / Eric Nathan; p10 © AAI FotoStock SA / Alamy / Geof Kirby; p12 © Forestry South Africa; p14 (left) © Lev / Fotolia; p14 (right) © vik173 / Fotolia; p16 (top) © Mondi; p16 (bottom) © Sappi; p18 © Gallo Images / Getty Images / Shelley Christians; p20 © AAI FotoStock SA / Science Photo Library; p22 © Alexander Potapov / Fotolia; p23 © macrovecto / Fotolia; p24 © AAI FotoStock SA / Florian Kopp; p26 © Mondi; p28 © Elite Photo Agency / AP Images / Kevin Woster; p30 © Sappi; p32 © AAI FotoStock SA / David R Frazier; p34 © AAI FotoStock SA / Alamy / Dan Lee; p35 © Mondi; p36 (top) © Guy Stubbs / Independent Contributors / Africa Media Online; p36 (bottom) © Mondi; p38 © Mpact; p40 © vivoo / Fotolia

The author would like to thank the Paper Manufacturers Association of South Africa, the Paper Recycling Association of South Africa and Forestry South Africa for reviewing the manuscript and for supplying additional information.

1 3 5 7 9 0 8 6 4 2

Contents

Paper is useful stuff..5
Where does paper come from?..7
Natural forests..9
Commercial plantations..11
Where are the forests?..13
Types of trees in plantations..15
Hard wood and soft wood...17
Forest fires..19
More about wood..21
Inside a tree..23
Growing trees for making paper...25
Harvesting the trees...27
Removing the bark..29
Making pulp...31
Whitening..33
From pulp to paper..35
Cutting and packing..37
Recycling...39
Word help..41

Many things we see and use every day are made from paper.

Paper is useful stuff

Most people use paper every day and do not even think about it. But how would we live without it? At home we read books, newspapers and magazines made from paper. We use tissues and toilet paper. In schools and offices, people draw and write on paper. In shops we see things packed in boxes made of cardboard, which is a thick kind of paper.

South Africa has lots of open space where trees can grow.

Where does paper come from?

Paper is made from wood, and wood comes from trees. South Africa is a big country. There are some big cities, some smaller towns and many small villages. But in between there is a lot of land. Some parts of this land are covered with trees. These areas are called forests.

The Knysna forest in Western Cape is one of the largest natural forests in South Africa. The trees make a safe home for the many animals and birds that live there.

Natural forests

Trees have grown in some areas for a long time. They have grown there naturally, and were not planted by people. These areas are called natural forests. There are different kinds of trees all growing together. Natural forests are important because many plants, animals and birds live there. Some of these cannot be found anywhere else in the world.

This baobab tree has grown naturally in Limpopo for more than 3 000 years.

A commercial plantation in Eastern Cape. Wood is used for making many things – furniture and parts of buildings such as doors and window frames, and also for making paper products.

Commercial plantations

In other areas people have planted trees to produce wood. These are man-made forests, called **commercial plantations**. In these forests, the trees are usually all the same kind, and they are arranged in straight lines with equal spaces between them.

Word help

commercial plantations: large areas of land where people have planted trees to produce wood to sell

South Africa has laws to protect natural forests. So all the wood used to make paper comes only from commercial plantations.

A map showing the main forests in South Africa.

Where are the forests?

The forestry **industry** is important in South Africa, because it employs many people. Most of South Africa's commercial plantations are in KwaZulu-Natal and Mpumalanga, but there are also plantations in Western Cape, Eastern Cape and Limpopo.

> **Word help**
>
> **industry:** all the businesses, people and activities involved in producing a product or service

A eucalyptus tree.   A pine tree.

Types of trees in plantations

The main types of trees grown in plantations are eucalyptus (we say: yoo-ka-LIP-tis) trees and pine trees. These trees are not **indigenous** (we say: in-DI-jer-nis) to South Africa, but were brought here from other countries.

> **Word help**
>
> **indigenous:** living or growing naturally in a particular place

A plantation of eucalyptus trees.

A plantation of pine trees.

Hard wood and soft wood

Eucalyptus trees come from Australia. These fast-growing trees produce wood that is quite hard. They can grow to be 50 metres high.

Pine trees come from North America and Europe. They can grow up to about 30 metres tall, and they provide softer wood.

Both kinds of wood are used to make paper.

A helicopter dropping water on a forest fire in Paarl in Western Cape.

Forest fires

Fires can destroy a whole forest very quickly. This causes the owner to lose money, and also kills many of the animals and plants that live in the forest. Some fires start through carelessness, such as people throwing their lit cigarettes onto the ground. Other fires are caused by lightning.

Workers clear strips of land in forests so that fire cannot spread so easily. They also keep a watch from high towers in the forest to spot fires starting so they can control them as soon as possible.

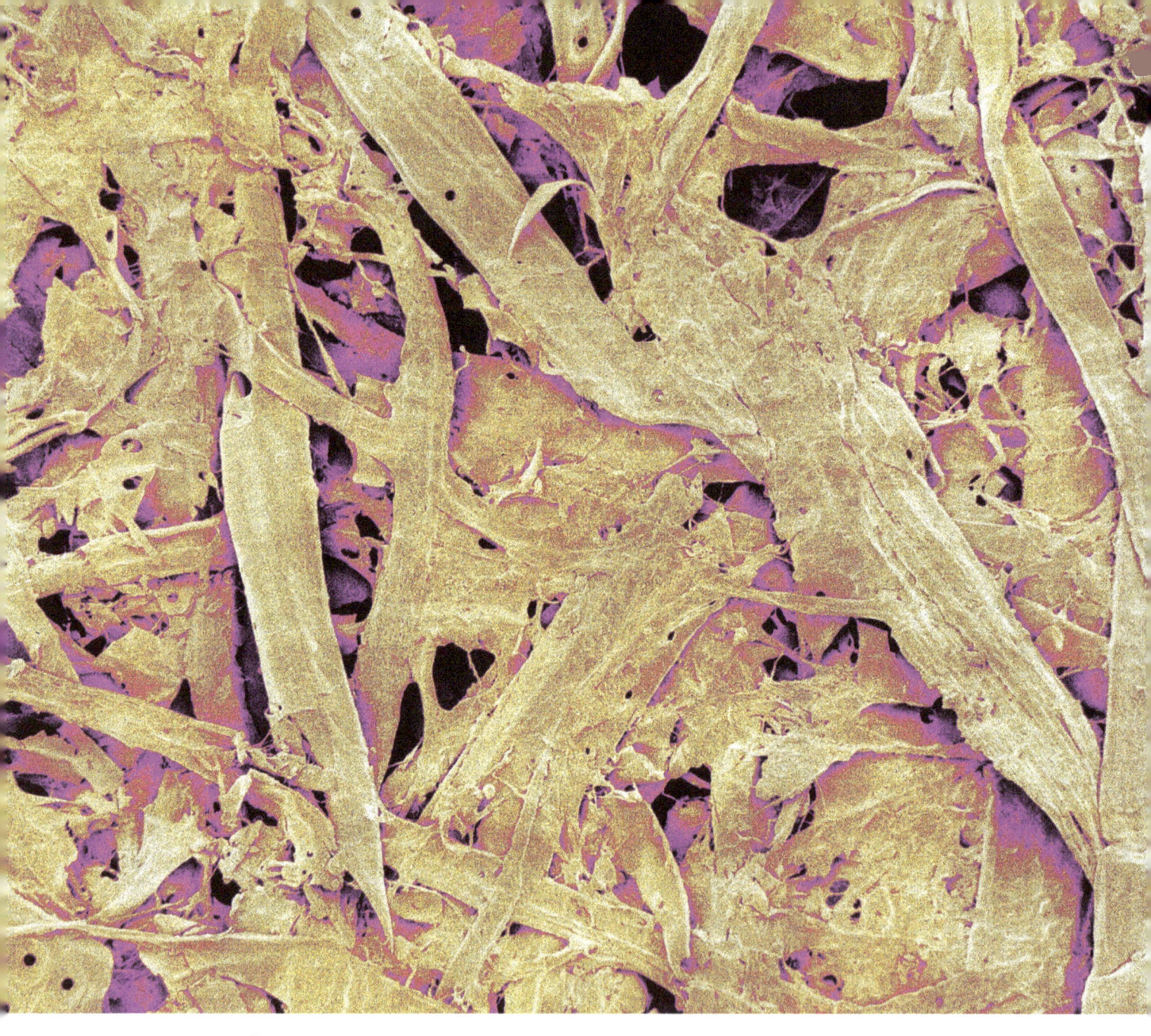

This picture of paper taken using a microscope shows the strands of cellulose.

More about wood

Trees are made of wood. Wood is made of fibres, which are thin strands of a material called cellulose (we say: SELL-you-lows). These fibres are held together with a kind of natural glue called lignin. This cellulose is what makes the wood so strong.

Paper is made from these cellulose fibres.

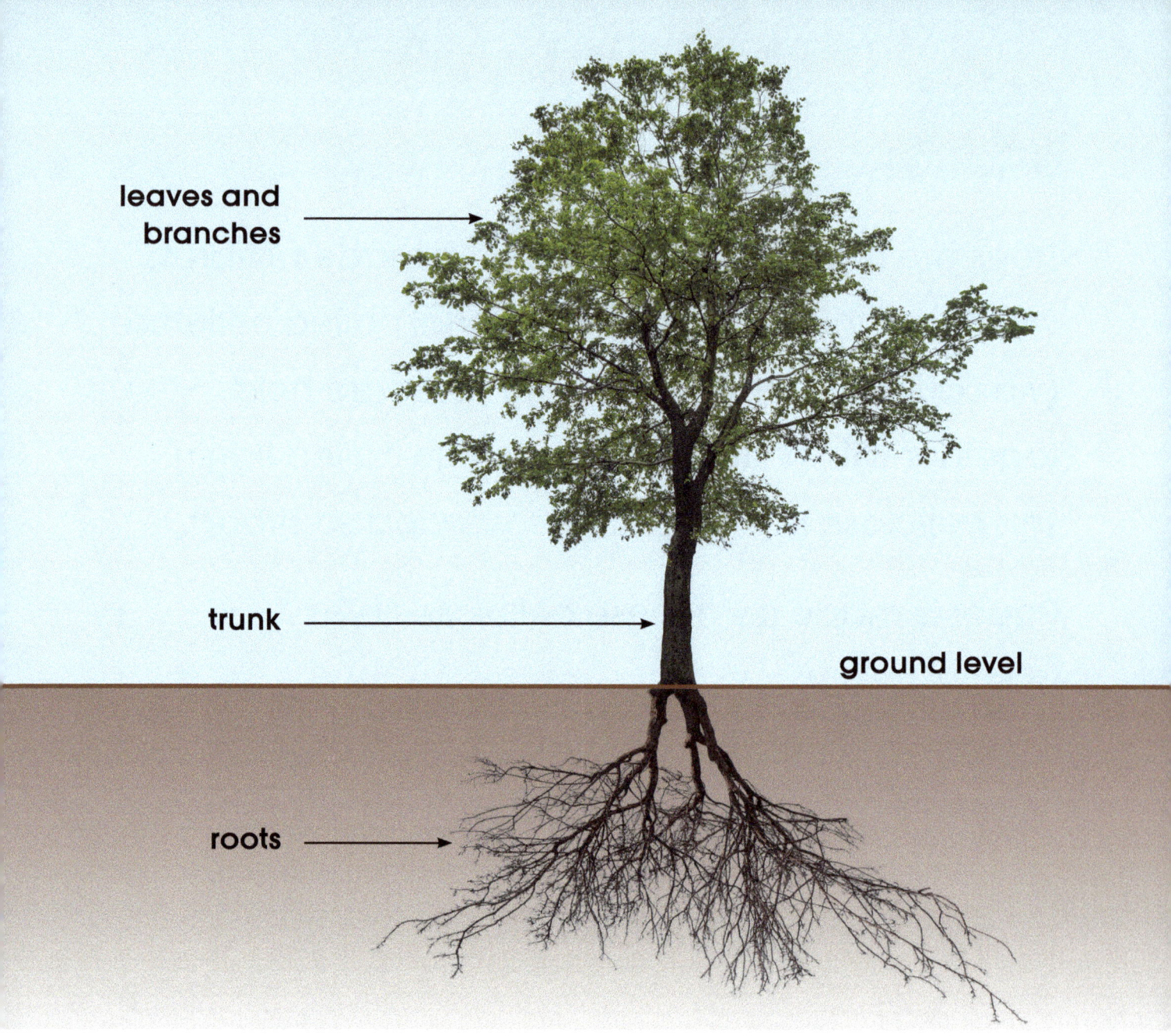

Inside a tree

If you look at a tree trunk that has been cut across, you can see some circles, or rings. The tree grows from the inside outwards. It takes about a year for a tree to grow one new ring of wood. So you can tell by counting the rings how old a tree is. Each year that the tree grows, the trunk gets wider and taller.

The outside of the tree trunk is covered in bark to protect it. The sapwood carries food and water through the tree. The heartwood gives the tree strength to stand up and grow.

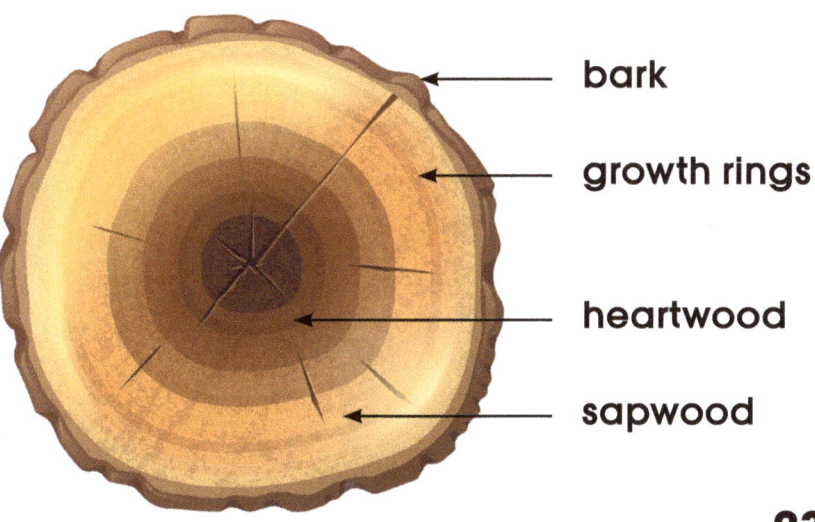

bark

growth rings

heartwood

sapwood

23

New trees are planted after the old ones have been harvested.

Growing trees for making paper

In South Africa, the wood for making paper all comes from trees that were planted in plantations. Plantations are like tree farms. Some farmers plant crops such as maize and wheat, and **harvest** them to produce food. Some plantation owners plant trees and harvest them to produce wood for making paper.

> **Word help**
> **harvest:** to gather crops when they are ready

After the trees are harvested, new young trees are planted.

A worker using a large machine to harvest trees in a plantation.

Harvesting the trees

A plantation is divided into areas called blocks. Each block contains trees that were all planted at the same time, so they are all the same age. When the trees reach the right age, all the trees in the block are cut down and sent to the **paper mill**.

> **Word help**
> **paper mill:** a factory that makes wood into paper

A large machine taking the bark off a tree trunk.

Removing the bark

The first step after the trees are cut down is to take off the bark. With eucalyptus trees this is usually done by workers in the forest. With pine trees it is done by machines in the mill.

This bark is not wasted. It is burnt in a boiler at the mill to produce steam and electricity, which are used in the mill.

This wood has been cut into small chips, ready for making pulp.

Making pulp

The wood fibres in the tree trunks are then made into **pulp**, which is a mashed-up mixture of fibres and water.

> **Word help**
>
> **pulp:** a mashed-up mixture of fibres and water that looks like porridge

This is done by first cutting up the wood into small chips. Then adding the wood chips to hot water and cooking the mixture until it looks like porridge.

The wood pulp is bleached to make it white.

Whitening

The pulp is a brownish colour, so before it can be used to make paper it needs to be made white. This is called bleaching.

Then the pulp passes through a machine that squashes it and twists the fibres together. This helps to make the paper strong.

The paper machine has many parts that change the pulp into paper.

From pulp to paper

Next, the wet pulp goes onto a paper machine that has lots of big rollers. This is called the wet end.

The rollers squeeze out the water and form the paper into one long sheet. The dry sheet winds onto a large reel. This is called the dry end.

In this part of the paper machine the fibres are squeezed between two rollers to make a long sheet of paper.

The large reels can hold up to 80 kilometres of paper.

Circular knives are used to cut the large reels of paper.

Cutting and packing

The paper is cut up in different ways, depending on what type of paper it is. Large circular knives cut the large reels of paper into smaller reels. Cutting machines then cut the paper into sheets.

Then the paper is wrapped, to protect it, and sold. Some paper is sent to factories to make cardboard boxes and packets. Other paper is used for newspapers, magazines and books.

Used paper can be made into new paper and cardboard.

Recycling

Paper is recyclable. This means that it can be used again. Instead of throwing away your old newspapers, magazines, boxes and milk cartons, you can collect them for recycling. Find out more about where to send paper for recycling where you live.

The old paper gets made into pulp again. Then it is cleaned to take out dirt, ink and glue, and made into new paper.

These bins are for people to leave old paper and cardboard to be recycled.

Word help

commercial plantations: large areas of land where people have planted trees to produce wood to sell

harvest: to gather crops when they are ready

indigenous: living or growing naturally in a particular place

industry: all the businesses, people and activities involved in producing a product or service

paper mill: a factory that makes wood into paper

pulp: a mashed-up mixture of fibres and water that looks like porridge

www.ingramcontent.com/pod-product-compliance
Lightning Source LLC
Chambersburg PA
CBHW051259110526
44589CB00025B/2882